How to Blog, Work, and Still Have Time to Clean the Bathroom.

(tips for new bloggers that want to do it all)

Inessa Radostin

Text copyright © 2016 Inessa Radostin

Photography copyright © 2016 Chris Vassalos, Inessa Radostin

All rights reserved. No part of this book may be used or reproduced in any manner whatsoever without written permission except in the case of brief quotations embodied in critical articles and reviews. For information address Inessa Radostin:

contact @inessaradostin.com

www.inessaradostin.com

Radostin, Inessa.

How to blog, work, and still have time to clean the bathroom: tips for new bloggers that want to do it all / by Inessa Radostin.

ISBN-10: 1533042497

ISBN-13: 978-1533042491

First Edition

WHEN IN DOUBT, CLEAN.

CONTENTS

INTRODUCTION ………………………………………………….. 8

CHAPTER 1: There's Nothing Good on TV, I'm Starting a Blog! ….................. 12

CHAPTER 2: Working Nine to Five, What a Way to Make a Livin' …………..... 21

CHAPTER 3: Delegating Like a Boss ……………………………………… 32

CHAPTER 4: Picture Perfect ……………………………………………….. 43

CHAPTER 5: Tips You Can't Put in Your Piggybank ……………………. 56

CHAPTER 6: The Work/Blog Mixtape ………………………………….. 64

CHAPTER 7: Clear Your Mind One Squat at a Time …………………… 71

CHAPTER 8: The Sweeter Things ……………………………………….. 84

CHAPTER 9: Get Over Yourself ………………………………………….. 98

ACKNOWLEDGEMENTS ……………………………………….. 104

RESOURCES ……………………………………………………... 106

FAVORITE POSTS ………………………………………………....... 112

ABOUT THE AUTHOR ……………………………………………. 122

AUTHOR LINKS ………………………………………………….. 124

FASHION CREDITS ……………………………………………... 126

INTRODUCTION

A while back I started my first blog. I was still working full time and needed an outlet for my thoughts: a diary slash hobby of sorts. The idea for the blog was to nurture my love of fashion, writing, and other daily activities that I had often shared with my friends. Shortly after I published my first article, I became engulfed by the notion of blogging. I was an addict and the blog was my substance of choice. As my efforts in developing a better platform grew, so did the platform itself. It broadened in topics and gained readership which only meant one thing– I needed to develop blueprints for a cloning machine so that there was one of me posted at my full time job, and one running the blog at home. I wish I could tell you that this book is about my success in creating such a machine but alas, mama did not raise a scientist! Instead, I've managed to find loopholes and small means of balancing the two while still giving myself time not to miss out on life.

A few months into blogging, I found myself stressing over miniscule details. A kitchen sink left full of dishes, the wrong coffee order, the toilet not being as clean as it could be. All of these things would drive me insane! The only thing that changed in my life was the blog and this was supposed to be a remedy to boredom, not a creation of yet another problem! Something had to change or I would forever lose the project I had so desperately wanted to succeed. What I quickly realized was the something that needed to change was me; more specifically my habits.

This book is a collection of what I've learned from operating a blog while also operating a full time career. It is not all parties and tiaras, a lot of it is hard work. The tips and tricks in the following chapters are some of the ones I have found to be most useful in creating a blog/work/life balance. Turns out that if you like things just so, starting a blog can actually make you go crazy. What you'll find in these pages are some of the points that worked for me (and have kept me out of that darling white jacket with the arms that tie across the back.)

A mix of advice to balance the madness, tips on blogging on a budget, sprinkled with anecdotes from my own experience in the blogging world; this book is the result of a bloggers journey in the online world. If your fridge is empty, your laundry is overflowing, and you're pounding at the keyboard then you, my dear, are most definitely a blogger. Not to worry, there is hope.

And trust me, that toilet won't clean itself no matter how much you will it to.

CHAPTER 1

There's Nothing Good on TV, I'm Starting a Blog!

Writing a blog: How hard can it be, right? I mean, depending on the subject of your blog, all you need is a camera, a computer, and a few ideas for some articles. If Carrie Bradshaw can make a living writing about relationships, why can't you make a living writing about shoes you like? What all the bloggers gallivanting across social media don't show you, is how much work starting and continuously working on a blog can be. If you're truly serious about your blog, you can say goodbye to your nights of Netflix and chill, and say hello to nights of "why the hell is this link not working?!?" What's more is, whether you like it or not, the world of technological advances is about to become your best friend, the kind who makes fun of you behind your back and tells everyone in school about that time you threw up on your shoes in gym class.

So let's start at the beginning: choosing your platform. If you're savvy with coding and creating sites from scratch then all the power to you. If however, you still think "Java" is a hipster way of saying coffee, then you will definitely need to sign up with a template creation website. There are people out there who can actually create a template website for you from scratch, then hand over the reins, for a certain price. But at the end of the day you will still need to teach yourself how your chosen template functions, so why not take control from the start?

When I was first choosing a site to run my blog from, I narrowed it down to three main choices. Each had pros and cons but after many weeks of consideration, I ended up choosing Squarespace. It offered the ease that Blogger offers but with a lot more customization options, and had less coding and complications involved than WordPress. This worked well enough for me; I was a novice who did not know much about online platforms. (If I were to be faced with the same option today, I would definitely give WordPress more consideration as I can now navigate through it far more easily.) However, if you're new to the world of blogging then Squarespace is a good platform to start with. It has a large selection of user friendly templates and you can choose to switch your template at any time with minimal work. (This is especially great if your blog develops quickly and is due for a re-brand.)

13 | HOW TO BLOG, WORK, AND STILL HAVE TIME TO CLEAN THE BATHROOM

The current look of the blog. It took four re-brands to get here.

Hashtag Learn From Your Mistakes.

The great thing Squarespace offers, which was incredibly appealing as a first time blogger, is that signing up for a yearly subscription gives you a choice of your own special domain (now you can look super professional when you start applying for all those unpaid jobs), and a personal email at your domain through Google mail.

So you've chosen your template and sworn on the stand with your hand on your credit card: Now it's time to begin designing the look and feel of your new aspiring online destination source. "But wait," you might say, "I haven't picked a name yet!" Not to worry, all will come in due time, grasshopper! Picking out a name before you even decide what your landing page looks like will limit your design options. If you already have a name in mind, you are more likely to have a notion of how you want it to appear on your site which is why I definitely recommend going through some of your favorite blogs and jotting down what you like about them.

These are just from the last couple of years.

Obsessive note taker much?

Then go through that list and figure out what works and what doesn't for the direction you want your blog to take. (This is assuming that you have already narrowed down what you want to share with the world, otherwise why would you start the blog in the first place, right?) Try to envision your site in your head: What color is the background? Is the font swirly or robotic? Where is the navigation located?

Write down everything you see. This may sound unnecessary, but when it comes down to editing your template, it will be helpful to have all of this covered *before* you're fifty articles in, and realize that you can't add a pop-up where you want it (and I am of course speaking from a sad and disappointing experience). If you've chosen to go with a template editor site to run your blog through, then use their sample material to see what the vision you had of your layout will look like on a computer screen. If you are starting from scratch then definitely throw random text and images into the mix so that you can see how your blog will operate once live. Oh, and don't forget that we live in the world of cellphones; make sure you check how your site will load on mobile devices. More often than not, a large percentage of your readership will be cell-based as that is where readers will be redirected when using social media apps. It's important that they see exactly what you want them to see.

Now it's time for the fun part, and by fun part I mean the self-deprecating, decision-making, over-analyzing-for-weeks part– the name of your masterpiece. Depending on the direction you want your blog to go, you might already have a name in mind. If you do, make sure you run a search on it to avoid doubling up on someone else's idea. If you don't have a name, I would do the same thing you did with your layout ideas: Start writing down anything that comes to mind, the more the better (this is not Thanksgiving dinner and your mom won't yell at you for not keeping your mouth shut!) Write down every word that comes to mind and when you're stumped, throw a thesaurus into the mix and write down some more.

Try to keep the name fun, but also consider what it will look like online, in a logo, in print, and as a domain name. When I was originally picking a name for my blog I thought I had it all figured out, and six months into live operations I decided that the name was too complex and did not work well online. This change of heart was a huge pain in my backside as I now needed to not only change my domain and anything that linked to that domain (internally and externally) but I also needed to change all of my social media accounts and print new business cards. Like I said, huge pain in the backside. Once you do choose a name you can see yourself saying about a hundred times a day (network, network, network), run a search on that name and anything similar to that name to make sure you are the only one who will be using it. Then go back to your site and solidify a domain name for that name (as now you have copyright of it online) and your personal email (something like info@yourdomain.com). You might be worried about going live with your site in order to buy a domain, but let's be realistic here; you do not have a readership yet and no one will know to look for your blog if you don't tell them to.

So look at you! You've got a template, a design, and a name for your blog. You're basically a rock star! Except for one small detail–content. As I mentioned before, you already know what you want to say, or at least who you want to say it to. Finalize who your target audience will be based on what it is you want to be blogging about: Will you be working on reviews for gadgets? Is it a beauty blog? Do you have a very surreal need to start a puppy blog? Whatever you choose to dedicate your blog to there is a large audience waiting to hear about it. The easiest and most inexpensive way to figure out who you should be targeting is by finding another popular blog that has similar subject matter and scouring the people who've left comments on their posts. Finally, our years of stalking our ex-boyfriends online will come in handy! Now you can stalk people online and call it "work"! Once you know your audience, it will be easier to tailor your articles to that audience, including using words that will appeal to them, and images that you know they will enjoy and respond to. When you finally start working on those articles, make sure you sit down and write a month's worth of material before you publish your first post. This will take some of the pressure off of having to produce material immediately, and will give you time to space out your articles. It is also a great way to buy yourself some time to get acquainted with your site because guess what? No matter how awesome you think you've made your layout, there will be a thousand details you'll want to change once you go live. When that publish button is pushed, consider the honeymoon phase of you dating your blog over. You are now in a committed relationship.

Let's check it out for a second: domain? Check. Site? Check. Content? Up the wazoo. So how come your metrics are emptier than your wine bottle after a tough day? We'll get to using social media to drive readers to your blog a little later, but at this early stage you should work on the page that will be a consistent landing page for anyone who stumbles upon your blog– your "About" page. Think of it this way; you're the new kid in the office and everyone wants to know what your story is. It helps that your story is amazing (otherwise you wouldn't be blogging), but who you are is not exactly written on your blog's metaphorical forehead. You need to introduce yourself to your readers and to search engines. Best advice I can give you is don't settle for some boring, overly professional sounding description of who you are and what your blog is. (This isn't a job interview!) You're a blogger now which means you are, above all things, a writer. To be a writer you have to have a style of writing. Your "About" page should be a slightly more toned-down version of the rest of your articles. Summarize the purpose of your blog, who you are (credentials help but don't be pompous, no one likes a show off), and why readers should stick around. Tell them what you have to offer. Be funny, be intelligent but above all else be who you intend to be in every other post you publish on your site.

Simply, this is how your online baby is born. You can now welcome it into the family, listen to its teenage wailings and pay for its existence with your hardworking blood, sweat, and tears. It will be magical! If you're worried about taking that first step into blogging, take a deep breath and a step back. This is not a job (at least not yet), so there is no way that you can mess it up. If you ever feel like pulling the plug then no one is stopping you. If you're still on the fence, then the only words of wisdom I can give you are the same ones that my mom gave me when I asked her if she ever regretted having a kid. She looked me straight in the eyes and said, "Inessa, you're a pain in the ass but in the end you've taught me who I am as a person. And I'd much rather talk to you than spend all day with your father".

CHAPTER 2

Working Nine to Five, What a Way to Make a Livin'

Unless your last vacation included climbing up a beanstalk and bringing back a golden goose, prior to your starting a blog you woke up each day and went to work. Whether you have a job that is quite demanding or an easy-going one, you now have to fit blogging into your schedule. Of course lucking out with a laid-back work schedule (because those must exist somewhere) means you will have a lot more time on your hands to squeeze some blogging into your day. If you're less fortunate and have a fairly demanding job, there are still ways to get both done without getting overwhelmed or sacrificing one for the other. The key to running a successful and headache-free blog is time. Much like going shopping at Costco on a weekend: If you can't be patient, get out of the store.

When your blog is still fresh it is very easy to become obsessed with it. In the first few months of owning my blog I went borderline "single white female" for it. I wanted to think, breathe, and dedicate every minute to it. While this is great for motivation, it is not as wonderful for either your sanity or your full time career. It is imperative to keep things in perspective when you first start out. While your blog one day may be the main source of your income, in its current, brand new state it is still only a hobby. If you knitted in your free time, would you jeopardize paying the bills to finish a scarf you've been working on? Probably not, so make sure you apply the same thought pattern to your blogging. There are quite a few bloggers out there who have abandoned any notion of a nine-to-five to run their blog as a business. While this is of course a possibility, starting a blog strictly as a money-making scheme is definitely the wrong reason. Not every blog succeeds and not every blog that does succeed creates revenue. By treating your blog as a business before it actually becomes one, you will likely do one of two things: exhaust yourself or exhaust your content. Going to work full time and spending every free minute perfecting your blog in an obsessive-compulsive manner will likely burn you out, and your blog will crash before you even have a chance to prove its worth. On the other hand, if you're running on rechargeable batteries and can function on a few hours of sleep every night (likely because you are a robot created in a secret government lab and set free amongst us mere humans, we hate you by the way), then redirect some of your energy away from blogging. At some point you will run out of material or begin publishing redundant information.

Let's assume that you are not a robot and are a pretty regular person with a full time gig that, demanding or not, still requires your regular attention. Having a nine-to-five certainly cuts into how much time you have left for blogging. (In the first few months of blogging I was fortunate enough to have a more lenient schedule with longer periods of off days.) However, even without a free schedule, there are still plenty of small things you can do every day to make some time for your blog. Find your free moments of the day and map out your free moment hot spots. Use regular lunch breaks to find a quiet corner somewhere and work on your blog. Avoid taking blog-related lunches at your desk if you have one. Not only is this highly unprofessional but it will also be unproductive as you'll likely be interrupted by nosy co-workers pretty regularly. If your workplace allows you to have ten or fifteen minute breaks throughout the day, don't let those go to waste. These are a great opportunity to catch up on your social media or respond to your readers. These days everyone is glued to their cellphones so you will not be singled out for pulling yours out on a break and not using it to play Angry Birds. (Not everything is about those chubby little freaks!)

Another good thing to consider in order to create more time in the day is to switch to commuting. I tend to get a lot of work done on public transportation (above ground with stable LTE of course). This is the time in the day when I can check my emails, catch up on correspondence, check in on social media, and even post material, depending how long my travels are.

Travel needs for every commute. No wonder my bags keep ripping.

The "commute office set-up" can be less than Zen, so definitely invest in a decent pair of noise cancelling headphones, unless you're working on an article about screaming children or that guy at the back of the streetcar who thinks everyone wants to hear about the issues he's having with his girlfriend!

Let's recap real quick: You're now working on your lunch breaks, checking your social media incessantly, and are commuting to work (because you care about the environment of course). You do not have a free moment to yourself and you trip over your feet pretty regularly because you're glued to the screen of your phone. Congratulations darling, you are a blogger! We've talked a lot about delegating time to avoid becoming overwhelmed. Much easier said than done, but not completely impossible, I'm sure you are incredibly excited about your new blog (single white female anyone?) Much like you would do in any other situation in life, make sure you only assign the amount of time to your blog that you know you will have available. Over-scheduling can very quickly lead to sloppy blogging. Instead, delegate an hour or two after you get home from work to everything blog-related. When I was still playing around with a schedule that would work best for me, I made the mistake of attempting to work on the blog after I'd had time to relax after work; at that point I was so relaxed that I had no desire to write or schedule any posts. All I wanted was a glass of wine, a blanket and a couch, but since I'd set up a session to write, I would force myself to do so. In a way I was setting myself up for failure; blogging should be something you enjoy doing. This is not a paid job (just yet) so it should never feel like you're working. After a few weeks of over-the-top poor writing, I decided to work on my blog as soon as I set foot at home after work; my mind was still active from the day and my energy was not yet drained. I was conquering my blog daily and not the other way around.

But what about the weekends? I mean there is no work then, so they must be a free-for-all, right? Not really. We'll go over making time for your personal life in a later chapter but as far as blog delegation is concerned I would recommend you schedule one full weekend day to writing and research, and use the other day for leisure. You will still feel like you get to have a break, but also have some serious hours logged into your blog. Saturdays are best for this because they're so close to your regular work hours, you can just ride out the hype of the week.

Now that you have your Sundays free for sleeping in, it's probably best you use the entire day. Ever notice how many under-eye concealer products beauty bloggers recommend? This is probably because they barely get any sleep, and guess what? Now that you have a full time job and a blog to run, you likely won't either.

Pretty much the best place in the world.

Before I started blogging I could easily get a full eight hours of sleep every night with the occasional ten hours on an extremely fun weekend. In the blog's first month of operation I think I got a total of ten hours for the entire week! Not only did this reflect poorly on my health but let's face it, I was a fashion blogger and could not spend hours Photoshopping under-eye circles out of every selfie. Much like everything else in life, the sleeping patterns of a blogger need to be planned out (are we sensing a pattern here?). After a few trial and errors (in this case the error of falling asleep half way on your bed with one of your heels still on), I've narrowed it down to the following regimen which seemed to work not only for my blog and job balance, but also for my own sanity:

6:00am: Wake up, wash face, coffee (key ingredient in this operation).

6:30am: Check emails, schedule posts, respond to readers (the fun part).

7:30am: Get ready for work or at least attempt to (thank god for top knots).

8:00am: Catch transit to work. Check all social media on the way.

9-5: Boring job (not the fun part) with the exception of a lunch break where I get to work on the blog (back to fun again!).

5:30pm: Transit home. More social media checks.

6:30pm: Researching or writing posts.

8:00pm: Dinner. Followed by passing out in a deep and uninterrupted stupor (followed by waking up with drool on the pillow and the cycle starts again).

Once you have a schedule set for everything (aside from bathroom breaks and the occasional personal freak-out, give yourself some freedom there), you can start using your full time job as a bonus as opposed to a nuisance. Don't think of the work you do for most of the week as something keeping you from your blog, but rather something that can help make it stronger. Are there connections you can make at work that can help? Depending on what you choose to blog about you should always draw from personal experience. So why not use your experience at work to help propel your blog further? Use any skills you may have picked up from your nine-to-five and transfer them to your blogging. Does your day involve communicating with people? Then use your well-developed people skills to reach out to affiliates and sponsors. If you work with computers, up your blog to a more visually-pleasing well-oiled machine. If, in the best scenario, you work in a field that is close to what you write about, then make sure you keep your business cards handy and talk to people who might be a good fit for your blog. The one habit I've developed and still keep up to this day, is to take notes of my surroundings, and quite often my notes prove to be useful when I am in a writing slump and need some fresh, out-of-the-box ideas for articles. As with anything else in your new life as a writer, you must document everything that you experience because you never know when those details will come in handy. Keep a journal at your work station at all times and take notes whenever you can. A sentence that takes you a few seconds to jot down can later become one of your most favored articles. Some bloggers keep their mobile voice recorders handy while others use Evernote and other note taking apps to organize their thoughts. For me it was always pen and paper; something about the feel of ink on a page made me feel all the more enthused, like I was actually a writer and not just another blogger in the mix.

This agenda holder saves my life on a daily basis. If it wasn't creepy,

I would give it a name and refer to it as a family member.

I guess we're all thinking it: Full time work sucks full time, and wouldn't it be great to just work from home and make your own hours? Well it sure would be, but in reality that is not the case for most bloggers, or at least it's not going to be straight off the bat. So maybe you hate your nine-to-five or maybe you love it. The point is to not let it affect how you feel about your blog. Set up parameters for yourself and have boundaries for the two, and try not to let your blog take over your work life. It will always seem like there's something better out there; to be honest, if I could quit everything I do and work in a candy store full time, I'd do it in a heartbeat but at the end of the day I'm pretty happy with all the balls I have to juggle. And let's face it, that candy wouldn't last a week with me in the store!

CHAPTER 3

Delegating Like a Boss

In the entire time I have run my blog it has very rarely felt like work, which is great and nothing to complain about, I'm sure. But my Eastern European roots are not able to stay completely positive it seems, and I see everything in my life through a magnifying glass. Peeping through this symbolic glass that is permanently attached to my psyche, I can say without a doubt that more often than not, working on the blog is exciting and fun. Yet there are times when it is repetitive and frustrating and well, work. Avoiding these parts of blogging is not realistic; you cannot be completely hands-off or your blog will no longer be yours, but will become very impersonal and extremely uneventful. With that said, there is quite a lot you can do to free some time for the more important, content-related parts of blogging, or for those nights of spending hours in your pajamas head-deep in a vat of ice cream.

Like mentioned earlier, there are certain actions you must take that need to be fairly manual. Aside from the writing itself, some social media apps have not integrated well with post-scheduling tools (we'll go over my favorite one later in the chapter) and, depending on the tools you are using, can actually require you to put in more time to delegate posts at a scheduled date. This defeats the entire purpose of online delegation; you're supposed to create less work, not add to the growing list of tasks you've already collected. I've found

Instagram and Snapchat to be the most demanding of all the main social media platforms. These two definitely require you to put some elbow grease in. While Instagram can be coordinated with other tools that you can run from your laptop or desktop, it works much better if you can publish your posts to this platform one at a time. Not only does this allow for better control of when your posts go out and the hashtags you use, but it minimizes the outside work of editing your images (which, much like the last ten Nicolas Cage movies can be painstakingly time-consuming with very minimal results.) The photo editing options on Instagram are directly geared to the app so why not use them to your best advantage? There are a large number of bloggers who actually document all of their images on their phones, so save yourself the money when you're starting out and don't spend thousands on professional camera equipment until you are at least five posts in and committed. If you're not a fan of filters then use the simple edit tools to get optimal results from your images on the spot. The Instagram camera allows you to avoid having to crop your image into that annoying little square after you've taken it, now you won't lose half of your photo to an unfortunate framing choice. Recently the app has begun to allow for full view images, which means you can upload images with any crop your little heart desires. But if you enjoy the continuity of the square format on your profile, you will still need to crop out some parts of your image to fit the layout.

Sometimes a good crop is all you need though.

When you're cropping your image, make sure to use the Golden Ratio or Rule of Thirds as much as possible. The general concept of it is dividing your image into nine imaginary sections via drawing two vertical lines and two horizontal lines evenly across the image. The important compositional elements are to land in the intersection of those lines.

In the case above, the ratio applies to the details of the handbag and the shoes.

The Golden Rule extends to the Rule of Triangles and the Golden Spiral. All of which function on a similar basis but with different visual divisions.

If you do not want the pressure of posting on the spot, and want to actually enjoy living some of your life, and post later, there are always options to get editing tool apps on your phone. My current phone editing go-to is a combination of VSCO®cam, Snapseed, Facetune, and PhotoDirector. I know it seems to be a lot of effort but the combination of the four gives me similar results to what I would get in Adobe® Photoshop® except it allows me to edit on the go. VSCO®cam is quite popular right now for its great filter selection and Snapseed and PhotoDirector are both wonderful editing programs with extensive options. For the most part I use Facetune to do quick touch ups like whiten teeth, remove blemishes, etc.

VscoCam

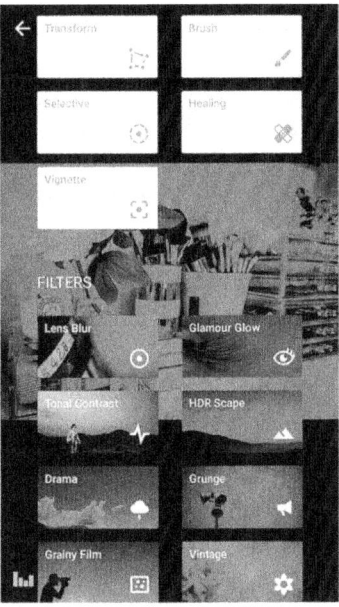
SnapSeed

FaceTune

PhotoDirector

The other platform I mentioned for being a manual time-stealing pit is Snapchat. If you use this app on your phone then you're aware of the fact that everything you do on this platform is temporary, and needs to be created basically on the spot. Essentially it is a mini broadcasting tool, so if you really have a lot of time on your hands, download the app and play around. I would recommend saving this adventure until your blog has a lot more traffic and you've grown your followers, so that the transition will be a more powerful one and you will not need to grow your following in yet another social platform.

Now that we've covered the complaint department concerning which platforms we cannot yet take off our plates, let's say hello to my all-time favorite time saving application: Hootsuite™. Basically what happened was millions of social media gurus got together, meditated, promised to sell their souls, and voila! Hootsuite™ was born. This tool that can be loaded to your laptop or desktop, as well as your phone or tablet, is an amazing source for online delegation. The initial view of the dashboard can be intimidating so I would suggest that before diving in you go through the Hootsuite™ University; these are tutorial videos that walk you through the program from beginner to advanced. The tutorials are easy to follow and best of all short, so you can get through a few at a time. After I downloaded the program, I watched all of the beginner tutorials and then just played around to set up my dashboard. Once set up, I could follow filtered feeds of all my social media accounts and repost directly through Hootsuite™.

But how is this any different from regular posting? Seems like a lot more work. Well, the best part is that you can auto-schedule all of your material. Any tweets, posts or pictures you might want to share can be scheduled (with hashtags) for a later time. You can either decide on the best time to schedule yourself, or let Hootsuite™ auto-schedule the posts for you at the most optimal hours. This is a great tool to have if you are working with a lot of affiliates; instead of taking an hour a day to post something on behalf of your affiliates you can now take some time once a week, or once every two weeks and schedule for the remainder of that period. I have found that, for myself, choosing the time for my original posts is the best option but using auto scheduler for posts I flip is a more beneficial tactic. This is likely because Hootsuite™ will already recognize the source, as it has been posted and reposted multiple times, and has a better chance of finding the optimal time of the day to promote the material.

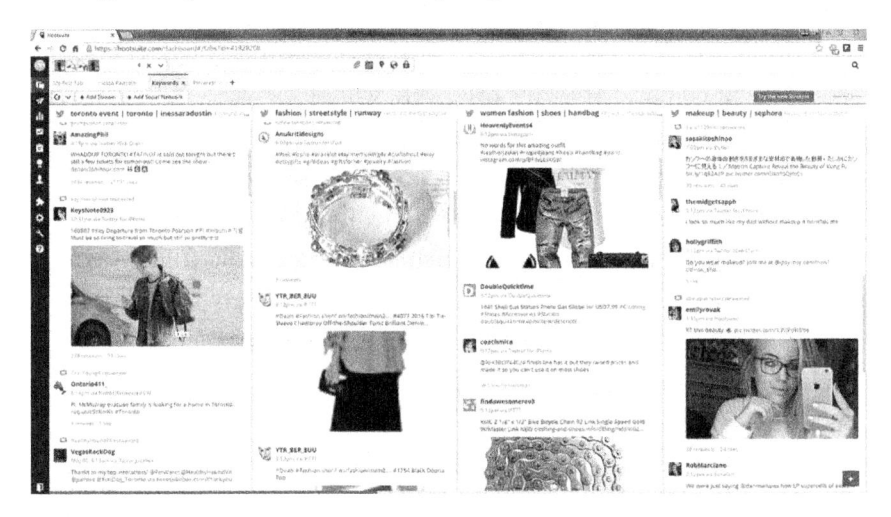

Hootsuite Screenshot

So why should you flip posts? I'm sure you're wondering why you need to use other people's materials when you're a big-time blogger now and have great articles leaking out of your ears. Well the truth of the matter is, it doesn't matter how good your material is, or how many original ideas you may have, people do not want to see posts about your blog all the livelong day. That can get pretty frustrating for readers and may cause you to lose followers instead of gain them. You want to keep the attention of the readers, but more importantly, you need to keep your credibility as a master of words and as an expert in your field. In order to do this you need to present yourself as being well-rounded and knowledgeable; better yet, don't just appear it, but actually become it.

Grow your interests in your field by signing up for a reading app. Apps like Flipboard (my personal choice) and Feedly give you the option of having news and stories stored on your phone to flip through and read at your own pace. You can customize your fields so that you don't get the latest news about water polo but only news of actual stories you'd be interested in reading (unless of course you love water polo). Because guess what? If you're interested in what you're reading, then chances are your followers will be as well. The best part of these reading apps is that they can be integrated with Hootsuite™ so you can auto schedule news stories to be posted on your social media networks straight from your phone. Once you have all of your accounts set up, you can choose which social media platform you want to post certain stories to, and choose the date and time for posting. I usually do this in the evening while having tea and watching some shows; it never feels like working, and realistically, I would have been on my phone regardless so may as well use it to get ahead in blogging! Programs like Hootsuite™ accommodate a large range of social media platforms. Most are free but some, such as the Tailwind for Pinterest integration cost money. Decide which social media platforms offer you the most response and make your decision on what you pay for from there. (When I started, I found that I had a lot accomplished without making any extra purchases on this program so save your money for when you absolutely need to upgrade.)

Now that you've found your salvation in online delegating, let's quickly go over the other ways you can help ease the workload of your blog. Creating articles can take up a lot of your time. There is research to be done, images to be taken and edited, then the articles have to be written, posted, and integrated with linkable material. There are clearly a lot of stages to putting a post together so why not break up the stages and multitask them with several posts? At the beginning of every week (or perhaps on that blog working Saturday you have), grab your idea book and settle on a few blog topics to work on. From here, do all of the research for each of those topics. Then take a few hours, or a full day if you have it, and designate it to image creation. This will include any photography you might need to do, or images you need to create from stock photos. This is a great option for product reviews since you can usually photograph a few products all in very similar set ups to save yourself some time.

If you're blogging about fashion make sure you always have your camera with you. Any time you have an outfit you can really sink your teeth into, ask someone you're with to take some photos of you and save those for your editing day, but make sure you alternate "friend photographers" to give them a break from your blog; chances are, they're there to spend time with you, not act as crew cast on a modeling audition.

Now that the images for all of your topics are in place you can set aside some hours for editing. Make sure you really give yourself time here; it's easy to get consumed editing your images, but it is also a very easy way to exhaust yourself with your own content. Give yourself plenty of breaks in between edits. After these few steps are complete, it's time to hit the typewriters. Since you already have the research down, and you're obviously passionate about all of the topics, you can fairly easily put together the written content for the posts. I find it best to write all of my content outside of the platform interface since it allows me to edit it a bit more easily, and because I'm used to writing in the familiar Microsoft® Word format. I then simply copy and paste my material into my blog's platform and add images, links, etc. Most of the top blog platforms will allow you to save drafts of your posts prior to publishing them so this is where the delegation comes in handy: Set yourself up to always have a few of these ready to go, so all you're doing is hitting the publish button on the days you'd like to go live with the article and share it to social media as it publishes. The beauty of using platforms such as Squarespace and WordPress is you can publish to several social media platforms straight from your blog as you go live. When you first begin to pre-prepare your articles in this way, it will be quite a bit of work, and the first few batches will be time consuming; but once you've loaded a few non-published posts into the back end of your blog you'll find that this system will actually save you a lot of time in the future.

I usually heave an internal sigh of relief when I manage to save myself an hour or two a day. When you're working a full time job and running a full time blog, every second really does count. At first, those extra steps in outsourcing my articles or delegating social media posts had felt like I'd climbed Mount Everest. A lot less sweaty and I didn't have a Sherpa but I felt as though I'd accomplished something! All those years I've spent on my phone were actually proving to be useful. I wasn't just checking my phone anymore, I was scheduling. It definitely took some getting used to and took a lot of personal reminders to get into the habit of being ahead, but once ahead I always managed to stay ahead. I found this was the best way to help myself work towards that full time job and blog balance: By putting in a little extra work on scheduled days, I actually ended up shaving off hours of work for myself that I could use at a later date, a day that was now free for me to use as I wished. Did I use that day to do absolutely nothing with my life and watch entire seasons of TV shows that I otherwise wouldn't have even known existed? Of course I did! Did I feel great about my blog while this happened? Absolutely. Did that feeling encourage me to find even more ways to find a balance for my work and blog? Hell yes.

CHAPTER 4

Picture Perfect

Whether you have screaming kids or screaming co-workers, starting a blog will require time management unlike any you've ever needed before! Consider a NASA engineer working on a deadline to build a piece of machinery that will trigger a rocket to launch in order to diffuse a meteor heading for earth and scheduled for impact in twenty four hours. This is pretty much your life now, minus the theatrics of doom, but time-wise basically on par. We've gone over a few things you can do to free some time in your schedule for blogging, but this blog of yours is not exactly going to run itself, so spending time on it is really unavoidable. The hardest part for me when I started out was to try not to feel like the blog was a second job; tough to do, as it takes quite a bit of work and will at some point actually create revenue.

What I found most helpful was treating the things I did for my blog as a hobby, and teaching myself new skills in order to do them. "But my blog is my hobby!" you might exclaim. Well sure it is, but that doesn't mean that you can't learn anything new in order to perfect your hobby. The two main skills that are most beneficial to a blogger (other than creative writing) are photography and video creation. Readers will want to see visuals on your site (especially if you are running a fashion and beauty blog) and not just lengthy articles; you're not working on the next *War and Peace* here. The words "photo" and "video" bring two things to mind— complicated and expensive. What I learned most from graduating from Photography Studies is that the discipline is really straightforward once you know the basics, and it can definitely be done on a budget. (I also learned that tearing up your old family photographs for a multimedia project will rain fire on your soul from your now very angry mother, but that is a story for another time.)

For the initial stages of your blog there is absolutely no need to run out to the closest camera store and purchase the most expensive, blogger-looking camera they have. I know there are a lot of flat lay pictures from bloggers showing off their tech, but you need to keep in mind that their blog is much more developed and has likely paid for their gadgets. One thing is for certain; you will most definitely need to invest in a camera at some point and when that time comes make sure you shop around before committing. There are a lot of options out for your choosing. Canon and Nikon both have a great reputation in the photographic community. You can buy a pretty standard body for these cameras for a low price. What you need to invest in is a good lens and that is where you can expect to spend some money. When I was picking out a camera to use for my blog, I went for the one that has the sharpest image, is user friendly (since a lot of times I'm handing it over to other people to get outfits shots), and is portable. This last point was very important to me as I am almost always carrying my camera and need it to be compact enough to fit in my purse. In case you're wondering, I ended up going with a Sony a6000 and I could not have been happier. Not only did it create amazing images but it had wonderful video capabilities which meant I did not need to purchase video recording devices or microphones when I started filming YouTube reviews.

So you've gotten yourself a new camera and have spent two weeks figuring it out. You've even taken a few shots that you thought were great, but now that you've transferred them to your computer they are just so-so. Now what? Looks like it's time to expand your new hobby! Photography and videography are nothing without editing. Post production is how you take your images from "so so" to "Holy crap! Did Man Ray take that for you???"! Most editing programs can be very confusing so I would definitely suggest you get yourself some tutorials online. For most programs there are also in-class courses available that you can take after work or on weekends but those can get pricey, and I'm sure you no longer have the free time you had before you started your blog. Online tutorials are much less expensive and you can learn at your own pace, no pressure. For your basic photography editing, Adobe® Lightroom® is your number one friend. You can get away with most edits with just this one program. It is fairly easy to figure out and is great for mass editing.

Adobe Photoshop Screenshot

If you want to step up your photography game by a few notches, put some time into teaching yourself how to use Adobe® Photoshop®. This is the main and most reputable program to use for photo editing. You can do anything from blurring backgrounds to slimming down your subjects in just a few minutes. (Hello extra portions of Chow Mein for dinner!). This is definitely a beast to figure out, so don't think you're going to be a pro right away. But it will definitely be worth the uphill battle.

Adobe Lightroom Screenshot

Once you're ready to get into making videos (if that is the direction you want your blog to take), Sony Vegas® Pro is my choice for editing. I have tried out quite a few, and this has been the most dependable and professional tool, and much less complicated than Adobe® Premiere®. When you're looking for editing programs, get a few trial runs and see what interface you're most comfortable with before you buy the full version.

Any photography you use in your blog should be as professional as possible. Readers are coming to you for expertise and knowledge and if your images appear sub-par, that will work against your validity as an expert in your field. Mainly, you will likely be creating images of products (unless you are a fashion blogger, in which case get used to not only being a blogger but also a model).

Not looking directly at the camera helps take the pressure off. I believe in this shot I spotted a squirrel and stared at it until it ran away. Then I pretended it was still there and stared longer.

Like a serial killer.

There are several ways to set up still life product photography, most of which can easily work on a budget. However, if you have access to professional grade lighting then by all means get them into your house and don't let them out of your site; these are your most precious cargo. When my blog started I had no access to proper lighting but more importantly I lived in a very small apartment and did not have the storage space required for studio equipment. What I ended up doing most often to capture product imagery, was to create mini studio set-ups around the natural light source in my space. I would set up full false vanities across from a large window and shoot when it was overcast out, to get the best diffused light.

Wait a minute, bed sheets are not studio grade backdrops?

Go figure.

Rainy days are nature's free light box. I have, on several occasions, used spare tile we had in the laundry room to create false backsplashes that on camera appeared better than anything we actually had at home. To save a buck, use objects you already have and rearrange them to suit your photography needs. Blog photography is all about staging.

At this point in our social media obsessed lives, YouTube is the mecca of our entire existence. This is essentially an encyclopedia of everything that we find interesting, or cute, or hilarious. There really isn't anything that happens in our life that does not somehow make it to a YouTube channel. (Remember that, the next time you trip and fall at the mall!) So, as a blogger, you would seriously want to tap into this outlet. Video creation can be a daunting task, especially if the only videos you've ever taken are the ones on your cell phone of your cat playing with your shoe laces. Until your blog brings in revenue, there is no need to spend money on your first video production.

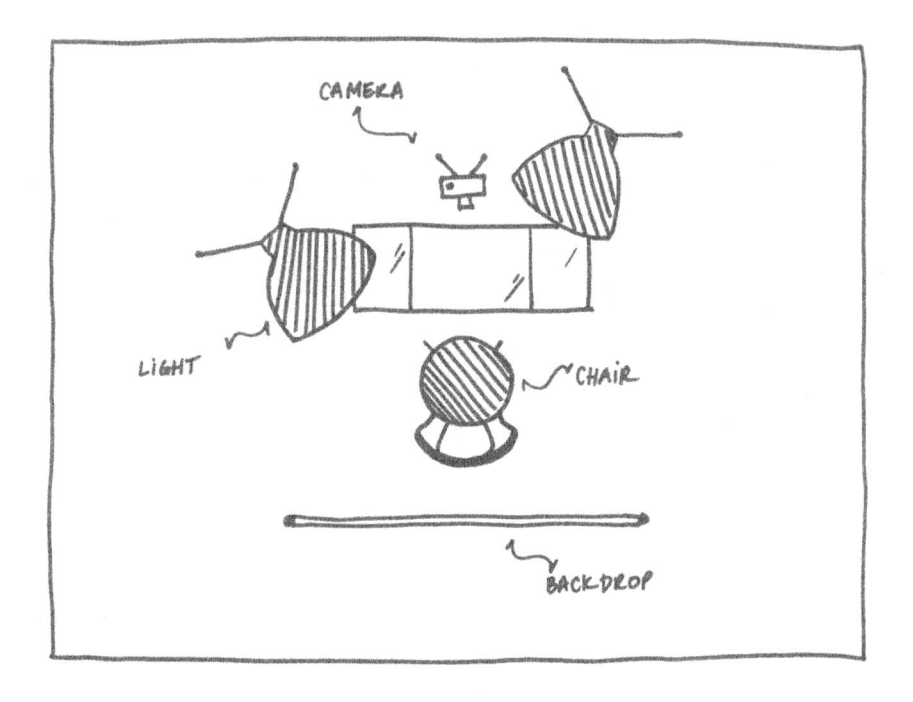

This is my basic video set-up. The backdrop is not always used depending on what I am filming. This is another way of saying that I don't roll it out when I'm feeling lazy.

For the first video I filmed I ended up spending a total of two hundred dollars and the only things I bought from a photo store were two reflective umbrellas for my lights. The lights themselves I'd actually adapted from two lampstands that I already had at home, white light bulbs from a local hardware store, and simple plastic clips to attach the umbrellas to the light stands. Since backdrops can get quite expensive, I purchased a thick, metallic fabric on sale in a fabric store and stapled one side of it to a long wooden rod (purchased for two bucks in a dollar store). Once the fabric was stapled, I used more plastic clips to attach it to two lighting tripods. (If you want to save even more money simply add hooks to the wooden rod and hang it directly from the ceiling or on the wall). Placing this super cheap set up across from a natural light source (similar to what you'd do with the product photos), will create a beauty light effect. This in itself saves you quite a bit of money as beauty lights can run upward of three hundred dollars.

HOW TO BLOG, WORK, AND STILL HAVE TIME TO CLEAN THE BATHROOM

What my dining room looks like when I film.

The cleanup makes me want to vomit.

When it comes to visuals, fashion blogging can be the most difficult to accommodate as you will need a lot of regular images of yourself and your outfits. Partnering with either another blogger or a friend who is willing to take photos of you is great, but as they likely also have jobs much like yourself, you cannot always expect them to have the time to help you out. In this case it's a good idea to take photos of yourself. Invest in a good tripod (one that is light enough to carry but is also sturdy) and pick some locations where you can shoot uninterrupted. That amazing photo of you in the middle of a busy street in your cute new shoes is a great idea but not reasonable if you have to set up your camera and run back and forth to take the image! Pick a few secluded locations where you have the space for full-body images and which won't have peeping toms making you feel rushed and uncomfortable. You can also purchase a wireless trigger remote which can be hidden easily in a pocket where it will not show up your shots.

Is there a shutter trigger in that pocket or am I just happy to see you???

Feeling camera shy? I sure was when I first started, especially when I tried to take images of myself outdoors. To get used to the idea, I decided to rearrange my home to create a more camera pleasing environment and I used that as an area to shoot my outfit photography until I felt more comfortable in front of the lens.

Whichever direction your blog will take (and trust me, like an overactive child it will not stay put) visuals will be a necessary evil that you will not be able to avoid. Consider yourself lucky; your new blogging hobby will lead to a new, visually-aware version of yourself! Once again, in the spirit of complete transparency, I will not lie to you and tell you that blogging is always fun. Though it is incredibly rewarding, there will be days when you will feel overwhelmed with how much you have to do, especially if your blog is in addition to a life that already involves full time work. For me, using photography as a hobby that accentuated the blog has helped me deal with those rip-your-hair-out days, because it gave me an outlet for the frustrations I sometimes felt with blogging. It was all very "Lion King circle-of-life" if you think about it: I started a blog to get a break from my career and got back to photographing to get a break from blogging. Both my blog and I have benefitted from the process. The images I have created not only elevated the general appearance of my blog and drove more traffic, but I had yet another thing to be proud of. I have in a very short period of time managed to succeed in my career, developed into a writer, and been able to pick up a decent amount of paid work photographing for other companies. (If I was only able to add "Unicorn Trainer" to my resume I'd say my life goals are fairly complete, so if you know of anyone who needs help with their unicorns, make sure to contact me directly!) In the meantime, pick up a hobby and give it your all; the unicorns will certainly follow.

CHAPTER 5

Tips You Can't Put in Your Piggybank

The day I wrote my first blog post I felt like I had succeeded at something special which generally made me the most awesome creature to walk the earth! That feeling subsided approximately one week later when I found myself to be more clueless than my grandmother that time we got her a Galaxy S5 for Christmas. Much like my (might I add now technically savvy) grams, I was pushing every button I could and trying every avenue of promotion wondering why nothing was happening (turn the phone on grandma...) I wish I had taken a bit of time to do some research on a few tips and tricks from bloggers who have already gone through this initial shock phase. Although I'm glad I had a self-taught learning curve, there are some pieces of advice that would have been useful to have known earlier on in my blogging career. The few tips you'll find in this chapter are the ones that helped me the most with keeping a work/blog balance, and that kept me from getting out-of-sorts with my blog.

Content sharing: This may be an obvious one. We all know that blog content needs to be shared in order to drive traffic and to get noticed on a regular basis. What most people don't know is that your blog site should make it easier for your readers to share your content themselves. You may not have a lot of traffic when you're starting out but any reader that goes ahead and shares your content is helping you by linking you directly to all of their friends and followers. They are not only your readers, but your very own marketing service, which is exactly why you should return the favor as much as you can. If one of your followers posts or shares or likes something of yours, it is only proper etiquette to do the same for their content. If you have time to share a picture of a kitten hugging a poodle and send it to half of your contacts, then you most definitely have time to show support for your dedicated readers.

Guest posts: These are your best foot in the door when you are starting out as a blogger. Do your research and see which other blogs or websites in your niche allow for guest blogging and get in contact with them. You don't need to send them a media kit so don't get overwhelmed with cold-emailing; a simple email with a few sentences, letting them know that you'd love to contribute to their site, will often do the trick. Make sure to include your site address, or better yet a few direct links to your best articles, in your email so that they have something to look over. There is a large number of blog sites that not only encourage but rely on contributing writers, and some are built based on this premise alone. Once you have a few articles out, a great idea would be to contact the editors of such online publications as The Huffington Post and see if you can guest-write for them occasionally. If they like your spunk then chances are you'll get a pretty quick response. Writing for other sites is a great way to get your name out there, meet new readers, and add a few more notches on your blogging belt.

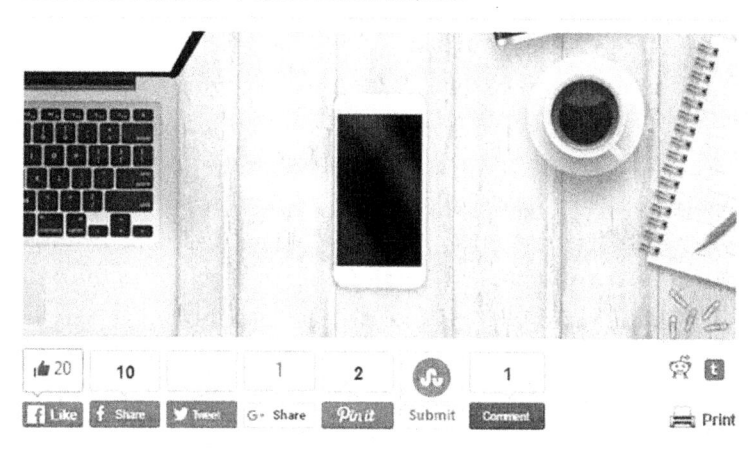

My first post for the Huff.

Build an email list: This is quite tough to do when you are starting out, as you don't yet have enough readers to encourage to join, but it is necessary to start this in the initial stages of your blog. Most people think that email lists are a marketing tool best left for product sales, but as a blogger, your email subscriber list is as important as any other social media integrations you might be working on, if not more so. Think of your email list as a means of delivering your posts straight to your readers' mailboxes. Those readers in response have a means to flip your email to their friends which in return may get you more readers. Develop an email list, if for nothing else than to keep in touch with your readership: to check in, to see how things are, and to make sure they know that you appreciate them visiting your blog. One of the better email integration tools that works well with most blogging platforms is Mailchimp. It allows you to not only create signup forms and pop-ups but to directly post links to your subscription boxes. A great time-saver if you ask me!

Don't be a copycat: Are there a million bloggers in the world who all look the same, publish the same articles, and have very similar-looking sites? Of course there are. Blogging is a trend-based occupation and much like everything that is popular, things that are trendy tend to get mass-produced. This doesn't mean that you can't publish material you enjoy or write about topics that interest you, simply because someone else might be doing it. It just means that you will need to do so in your own way and style without following in their footsteps. If you review gadgets on your blog, chances are that other people will have reviews of the same products, but they will not be using your voice to do it. If you decide to start a fashion blog, on the other hand, you will likely have images that look very similar to other fashion bloggers because let's face it, ever since fashion blogging became a thing, stores began to carry more and more similar-looking products. The point is, you might look like them but you definitely don't have to sound like them. Find your own voice. Speak the way you would speak to your closest friends and not the way you think you're supposed to as a blogger. If you're unsure of what that voice is (as I was when I first started out) then use your blog to help you find it. After a few articles you will know exactly what your writing style is, and from there work on developing that; and forget about mimicking what you see on Instagram just because it's popular. That would be a huge waste of your time.

Go to sleep on time: In the first few weeks of blogging, I stayed up until about three a.m. every night, trying to perfect a layout, working on images, or getting ideas together for topics. This not only made me exhausted during the day, and caused me to under-perform in my full time job, but it also jeopardized my blog, as I was actually working myself out of it. It's easy to get engulfed when you first start out but it's also just as easy to let go, shut off your laptop at a reasonable hour, and get some real rest. Working on your blog before you go to work is always preferable, as you're in a high-energy state (especially if there's a Starbucks involved) and you have fresh ideas. If you stay up late you are more likely to burn yourself out halfway through your day and lose potential blogging hours after work that you otherwise would've felt quite ready for. Your sleep is as important as your high end handbag; treasure it like it came in a dustbag.

Give stuff away: People love free stuff, it's undeniable. A good giveaway campaign can drive an immense amount of traffic to your blog and social media platforms and can be easily done on a budget. I'm not saying do your spring cleaning and throw the things you don't want into a gift bag, but you also don't need to rush to the big box store and spend hundreds of dollars on gear. A small giveaway can cost anywhere from nothing to under fifty dollars if you're smart about who you market it to. If you already know what your readers want, or think you do, pick up some items that might appeal to them. (Work these into a blog post and you're killing two birds with one stone.) If you're a beauty blogger, a giveaway is so simple it's mind-blowing, as you can definitely find a lot of beauty items for a fraction of the cost. If you don't want to invest the money (or you have readers with more expensive tastes) then partnering with one of your affiliates or some of the businesses in your local area might be a good idea. This way they can provide the swag and you provide the outreach platform; everyone gets more attention and everyone wins. To loop back into email list-building, implementing a strategy to get people to sign up for your email is a great way to get the giveaway to give as much as it can.

Network until your eyes bleed: Being a blogger means one of two things: you can either spend a lot of time at home in your underwear, or you can go out constantly and meet new people. I prefer the latter choice as it lets me have an excuse for needing new outfits but also because you never know who you're going to meet. I always make sure I have some cards with me when I'm out, and more often than not, they end up being handed out. Any social gathering you go to can lead to great opportunities for new bloggers. Small businesses are on a growth spurt at the moment and most of these businesses are looking for small, affordable marketing strategies. If you are still in the beginning stages of your blog then there's a good possibility that you will work in exchange for merchandise to review on your blog, so introduce that idea to people you meet who might have a product you are interested in writing about. Please don't walk around announcing to the world that you have a blog; life is not an audition, but do make sure that you slip it into the conversation if it is appropriate to do so.

Keyword searching: A must. An absolute, time-draining but totally worth-it must. I was knee-deep in articles before I asked myself, "Why on earth are the fruits of my labor not showing up in searches???" (I asked this in a much less calm tone, and with a lot of rather inappropriate language! But I asked it nonetheless.) The answer was quite simple: I did not invest my time in keyword searching. Much like most new bloggers, I was naive enough to believe that my material would be enough to help push my blog ahead of some others. Boy, was I way off! No matter what we like to believe, people are not spending their days looking for our blogs. You have a few measly seconds to grab your reader's attention and that's all you have until they flip over, or scroll through, or shut you off entirely. To make the most out of these precious, attention-grabbing seconds, you need to make sure that you are using the language your reader is speaking, or in this case, reading. For any blog title, tag or tweet, make sure you run a keyword search to see what readers are looking for. The Google Keyword Tool is a great little helper but I found for me what works best is simply typing the words into a search engine and seeing what websites pop up. Instagram has a great tool embedded into the platform that shows you the number of people using your hashtags, and if you're into vlogging, enter your main words into YouTube and see which suggestions come through. Whatever your research system for keywords, make sure you use both popular and less-known words. While tagging your posts with highly used keywords will likely get you more traffic, using the less common tag words and phrases will allow you to tap into a more "niche" audience which usually brings with it a more dedicated readership. Now that you're a blogger, words are your weapons but keywords are your weapons on two Redbulls and a Venti triple shot latte!

Show support: Treat other bloggers as comrades in the same battle and not as competition. Whether they are more successful with their blog than you, or are just thinking about starting a blog, anyone willing to get into this business knows what you are going through.

They have had the same issues and successes as you have had and for the most part are really great people if you give them a chance. If someone is asking you for advice on blogging, don't turn them away and don't act high and mighty; one day you might have questions of your own (if you don't already). The bloggers with the most success in the field have developed very close friendships with other bloggers, and help direct readers to multiple blog sites. Talk about hashtag squad goals, right?

There are a lot of tips for new bloggers circulating in blogging circles. These are the ones that I found most accessible and most beneficial to me. They became almost a mantra and a routine of sorts, while blogging became a way of living. Once you have your blog lifestyle figured out, the remainder of the work comes much quicker. Following some of the tips I've mentioned will help you free yourself of wasted time in the future. Oh, and if you can, use some of that time to help your grandma figure out the icons on her cellphone. You never know, one day you might need her to take a picture for your blog!

CHAPTER 6

The Work/Blog Mixtape

This chapter is a more in-depth discussion on how working and blogging can be mutually advantageous. I had always wondered about how great it would be to somehow combine a full time job with a blog. Like, wouldn't it be great if my full time work could propel my blog and vice versa? Mostly that question fell into the same category as wouldn't it be great if I was just walking down the street one day and found a genie lamp? After about a year into blogging I realized two things: My work and blog could be intertwined minimally but effectively and even if I did find a genie lamp I would likely squander all my wishes at the nearest Chanel store. Instead of wishing for unrealistic pursuits I began to use aspects of my full time career as a collaborative effort towards the blog. Plus, I quickly found out that there were things I did (not at work but outside of it) that were actually useful for blogging; things that I took for granted and assigned to the category of "work" instead of the category of blog.

Working in an office-based environment, there is a very good chance that you attend certain events that your office puts on. It might not be a weekly ritual and scarce as they may be, these events can be quite useful to your new and flourishing blog. If you are a lifestyle blogger then the obvious choice is to document the events and write about them on your platform

Runways are a huge plus if you're in the fashion industry. Wear sturdy shoes though, my feet were trampled by some serious stiletto stabs by the end of the night. Awesome.

But how do you use your workplace outings when your full time work does not closely relate to your blog's niche? Quite simply, you use it for your social media to drive traffic to your blog. It might be exhausting to take a million pictures while you're trying to enjoy a night out with your co-workers, but your readers and social media followers want to see who the person behind the words they read really is. Don't be ashamed of having a full time job: Be proud of it! Your professional life might not include regular trips to Bali but it will still include fun outings with interesting people. So take those pictures of your office lunches and tweet about your happy hour drinks; hashtag work life is nothing to shy away from.

While you're out and about both during your work week and after-work gatherings, don't be afraid to network. You don't have to announce to every person you meet that you're a blogger but make sure when you're meeting new people that you get their business card whenever possible. Never forget that your co-workers are also people who have friends, and if they like you enough, they can introduce you to people who will be of benefit to your blog. The key to successful networking is being a likeable person, not as a scheme but as a genuine representation of who you are. In the raw beginning of my blog, before I even published my first article, I had a multitude of conversations with people I worked with about it; not in any calculated way but simply to get advice and to catch up with the people I was spending forty hours a week with and to let them know what I was up to outside of the office. A lot of those conversations ended up as leads for articles; my co-workers forwarded my name to a friend who then forwarded it to their friend and so on and so on. When I mention networking to new bloggers I often get a certain response; they are usually fearful of self-advertising, thinking it makes them appear pushy and self-absorbed. What most people don't realize is that networking is not always a marketing ploy. Most often it is simply meeting new people, and if nothing else, you might find a good friend in the process.

A lot of blogging (especially in the lifestyle genre) involves product reviews. When you're starting out you might be tempted to purchase items for the purpose of leveraging them on your blog. Though I encourage this idea for later on, at this stage I would recommend starting a little closer to home so that you avoid paying for a hobby that is not yet paying you in return. Your blog might be in the exact same niche as your full time job; in this case, there is a very good chance that there are products that intertwine the two. If you review computer programs on your site, then pick one that you use at work. You are skilled and fully-trained in it so who better to have an opinion about it? I spent most of my professional career in the fashion business so when it came to starting a blog, it made the most sense to have it revolve mainly around fashion, with added subsections for other interests in my life. By doing so, I could easily tap into my excessive knowledge of the field from my professional life, and use that to form my blog expertise. Even something as simple as a new food item in the cafeteria can turn into an article; maybe you are a lifestyle blogger and your workplace has taken a new approach to organic food products. There's huge potential there for a great piece on green living! The main driving force behind good blogging is research. Consider your professional life as an untapped source of information in which you are already a guaranteed expert.

I've mentioned that you should use social media as much as possible when attending work-related events. Depending on the basis of your blog, you should do the same for your general work environment. I often tweeted about being at work during lunch hours and found that I had a great response to those messages. Keep in mind that most of your readers are also at work, and if you can catch them during lunch or right after their work day is over (much like yours), they are more than likely to peruse your blog. Instead of waiting for them to scroll through hundreds of updates to get to the post you published the night before, remind them that it's there when they are on their phones or tablets. While you're at it, throw in a few photos of your office space or an in-transit image of yourself. This way you're showing your readers that you can relate to their everyday life and are not just another blogger; you are a comrade-in-arms.

Online presence and social media is not something we can get away from and as a blogger you are more attuned to online social circles. Your co-workers are quite likely circling on the same social apps as you are. They might not be following the same sites, as yours are directly geared towards your blog, but they most definitely have online friends collected. Having your co-workers read your blog and show support could mean a very large traffic increase to your site. Consider this a dramatic privilege; you get to meet your readers face to face every day so keep them in tune with what you are doing, because if they enjoy your content then so will their friends. It is also important to listen to people you work with about who they might be following and who is grabbing their interest. In your new life as a blogger this is all in the spirit of professional research. Your co-workers might be able to lead you in the direction of a successful blogger in your niche, who you can learn from; they might even know that blogger personally. My first few months in blogging were a huge learning curve gathered directly from my full time job. Once I'd let people I work with know that I have a blog, I was forwarded a lot of names of other bloggers in the field, bloggers I still follow and keep up with who inspire me regularly. Having my co-workers also be passionate about fashion and lifestyle helped me pick their brains for the blog. If I had some knowledge in one field they had experience in another. Once I'd write an article that had spurred from a conversation with them, I'd let them know, or tag them in a social post to offer credit, which resulted in a lot of reposts and retweets.

Most bloggers get borderline-obsessive with a few main social media platforms. The most common blog geared apps of choice are Instagram, Twitter, Facebook, and Snapchat. Tumblr plays its hand as well, but for me those are the top four when it comes to pushing out content and generating research. The one forgotten platform that is a very useful resource for bloggers in LinkedIn. Working in a professional setting you probably have a LinkedIn profile. If you do not, get one going as soon as possible. A lot of people equate LinkedIn with a way of getting work, and why do you need another job, right? You already have one plus a blog; your plate is full. The next time you sign into your LinkedIn account scroll through some of your contacts. You would be surprised at how many of them might be interested in hearing about your new blog, as they might be in a field that is relevant to what you've chosen to publish about. Start adding connections on this site daily if you can. The fastest way to do so is to run a search for a profession that is in the niche of your blog's theme and connect with those people. You can later use those connections to message people in order to introduce the blog or to find affiliates. Don't be a spam monster because that's pretty annoying, but a friendly email can't hurt. Before you do any of this, of course, make sure your LinkedIn profile is top notch and includes your blog information. Get a professional headshot, comb through the work experience you've posted, and if you can, invest in a professionally created bio. These can run anywhere between fifty and two hundred dollars (depending on the length) but are a great investment. If you choose to write your own bio, do not make it overly whimsical as you would for your site; this is still a professional environment so it's best to keep it that way.

There will be some days when your full time work will not be entirely intertwined with your blog, and in all honesty that is for the best. Your blog is your "me" time so don't taint it with your "I had another awful day at work" time. But making some parts of your everyday job work towards your blog can actually relieve stress from work and add a level of multi-tasking to your days. The best thing I've done for myself since I started blogging was to allow moments of labelling myself a blogger when I was at work, and doing the same for my daily profession when I was working on the blog. This way I was never one or the other but the two combined, which let me see opportunity where I otherwise would not have seen it. People say that a work and life balance is the key to success; the same should go for a work and blog balance. So throw your job and blog in a cookie jar and shake it as hard as you can, mix them up, dough them in, and bake a freaking cake with the mixture. You're in it for the long haul now. Most importantly, no matter how you decide to find your perfect mix, never, and I mean never, stop looking for that genie lamp!

CHAPTER 7

Clear Your Mind One Squat at a Time

I am by definition a very lazy person; if given the chance I would gladly sit on my butt all day, stuff my face with pizza and candy, and only stretch to get rid of the numbness in my legs from lack of use. Working full time and running a blog helped me mask that laziness so that to the world I appeared to be motivated and energetic while deep inside the lazy kid in me cried out every time I averted my gaze from a twelve pack of donuts. In order not to completely fail at the goals I've set out for myself, and at life as a whole, I've adapted to include regular exercise into my week. The exercise I choose to concentrate on is not geared towards weight loss, or muscle gain, or any of the standard results one would expect from hitting the gym. I focus most of the regular workouts I do on creating some form of relaxation and mind-release while I am performing them, and that last for hours after I am done. I find that using some of the free hours I have in the week to incorporate short workout routines helps me direct my focus more. Don't get me wrong, I still work on mad cardio when I have a bit more time to spare, and especially closer to the summer bikini months (because I'm definitely a conditional exerciser), but for the most part I work on clearing my mind while also keeping my body fit. Once your blog begins to grow you will notice that you do not have the time to keep up the former hours you used to put into the gym. In fact you may not even be able to remember the last time you tied your running shoes, but making some time in your week for proper mind-clearing exercise will work wonders for your brain power. Now that you're a blogger you are held obligated by an unwritten rule to have fresh ideas for the sake of your readers' interests. Polish your brain the same way you'd polish your article edits and you'll never run out of innovative ways to entice your audience. In this chapter, you'll find a few of the exercise routines I use the most that help de-clutter my mind. They help me separate daily activities (such as a full time job) from blogging activities, and by performing them several times a week I am able to remove myself from the clutter of daily life. Added bonus: They keep the lazy, donut eating kid at bay one workout at a time.

Lunges

Great for allowing your mind to concentrate on form and as such, forget about everything else. Also great for that booty! Keep your upper body straight with your chin up and shoulders back. Step forward with one leg and lower your hips until both legs are bent at ninety degrees. Push back up to the starting position. For space constraints, do this in one spot while alternating legs. Repeat ten lunges for each leg four times over.

Spider Lunges

A good form of slow cardio that helps stretch the body. Position yourself in the same way you would if you were in a plank. Tighten your abs and slowly bring your left foot towards the outside of your left hand (bring your foot half way if you cannot stretch that far). Keep your right leg where it is. Hold this position for approximately two seconds, then slowly bring your left leg back to the original plank position. Repeat the same technique with your right leg. Complete ten full sets.

Walkouts

All aboard the killer ab train! This exercise is a combination of plank and stretching. Stand with your feet hip-width apart and bend over to place your hands on the floor directly in front of your feet. While shifting your weight to your hands, walk your hands forward. Keep your back flat and continue to walk yourself forward until you end up in a plank. Hold for two seconds and walk your hand back to your original position, then slowly stand up straight. Repeat ten times for three sets.

Side Lunges

A great workout for your inner thighs and backside (no need to sell this one any more…), but is also wonderful to train your inner and outer balance. Stand up straight with the knees and hips slightly bent. Take a step to the right; keep your feet forward and stay low. Extend the left knee and shift your weight to the right to complete the side lunge while keeping your head and chest straight. Pause for two seconds then use your right leg to drive you back into the standing position. Repeat the same on the left side. Repeat ten lunges for each leg four times over.

Planks

Well-known ab exercise that I find beneficial for meditation purposes. Start by getting into a push-up position. Bend your elbows and rest your weight on your forearms but not your hands. Your body should form a straight line from your shoulders to your ankles. Hold this position by counting to thirty slowly. Repeat three times.

Side Planks

Strengthens your back and helps with focus and concentration. Lie on your right side in a straight line resting on your forearm with your elbow directly under your shoulder. While tightening your abs, lift your hips off the floor but maintain the straight line in your body. Keep your neck in line with your spine and hold while counting slowly to thirty. Lower your body to the ground with control. Repeat three times on each side.

Arm Circles

Promotes circulation and stretches those tense typing muscles. Stand with your feet shoulder-width apart and lift your arms straight to shoulder height. Move your arms in a circular pattern in circles approximately six inches in diameter with your palms facing down. Continue to do so for one minute. Relax your arms for a few seconds, then repeat the exercise in the opposite direction. Repeat five more times in each direction.

Yoga Squats

This technique helps you control your breathing and allows for a more relaxed head space. Squat with your feet as close together as possible. Separate your thighs slightly wider than your torso. While exhaling, lean your torso forward and fit it snugly between your thighs. Press your elbows against your inner knees and bring your palms together. Hold this position while counting to forty, then inhale, straighten the knees and slowly bring yourself back into a standing position. Repeat five times.

Revolved Chair Squats

A favorite of mine from yoga practice that strengthens the legs, shapes the butt, and stretches the spine for increased relaxation. Stand with your legs hip width apart and lower yourself into a standard squat position. Exhale and twist your torso so that you are bringing your left elbow to the outside of your right knee. Press your palms together so that your right elbow points towards the sky. Stay in this position for five full breaths then unroll into the original squat and repeat on the other side. Stand straight and relax your legs. Repeat three times.

Bridge Stretches

Especially helpful if you are sitting at a computer for most of the day as it stretches your entire body. Lie on your back with your arms by your side and your legs folded with knees pointing upward. From here use your arms and legs to push your body up. Hold while slowly counting to five, then lower your body down. Repeat four times.

However busy your calendar may be, fitting in a short amount of time for exercise can help stimulate your mind and regulate your energy levels. If this means you'll need to pencil yourself into your own calendar, then so be it. Whether you sign up for the local gym or just perform these exercises in the living room right when you get home from work before you hit your blog list, spending any amount of time on short workouts will be one of the most beneficial things you can do for your blog. Now that you are blogging, you are spending a lot more time sitting down, which as comfy as it may be, is not the best thing for your health. It wasn't until I heard my father tell me that I looked unhealthy (in less soft-sounding terms), that I realized how obsessive I had become with spending excessive time on my work and blog. I had to re-evaluate my daily priorities and slowly work the exercising and meditation back into the schedule. Since doing that, I can multi-task with more ease and have a lot more energy throughout the day. Do I still have days when all I want to do is sit on a pillow on the floor with my laptop and not get up for hours? That's pretty much a given, but at least now I know my mental health can afford the binge break.

CHAPTER 8

The Sweeter Things

You know those "Home Sweet Home" door mats you see on the front stoops of some homes and you cringe? Well turns out they are not the worst. Just kidding, they're pretty terrible, but the message behind them is actually very important for bloggers who also work. There are only so many hours in the day and bloggers' hours are pretty full, especially when you are balancing a full time job and a blog. Making time for the people in your life becomes a scheduling nightmare when your calendar is ripping at the seams with chores! Your Home Sweet Home might not be so sweet if all you're doing is working yourself silly. It is definitely a more sour home if you've also moved your blog office into it. Now that you're a blogger, every room is reminiscent of your blog in one way or another: the bedroom screams for Instagram pictures, the bathroom aches for a blog friendly remodel, and what was once your dining room is now littered with laptops and paperwork. But what about all the things that made you happy before you started blogging in your free time? How do you get those back?

The saying 'family comes first' did not get its popularity for no reason; otherwise it would not be the center of nearly every cheesy coming-of-age movie. It might be easy to push your family to the side when you're busy building your blog brand, but keep in mind, they're likely the ones who supported you the most when you initially decided to start the blog. They might not be SEO savvy or great with a camera (although from my own experience, they'll be eager to learn if it means helping you out) but they are by far your biggest fans. More importantly, they are your best bet on feeling like yourself after you've taken off the work and blog hats you've been donning all week. I'd be lying if I said that I don't have days when all I want to do is cry in the bathroom and miss my mommy. On the plus side, I'm lucky enough to have my parents close by, so when I'm stressed I can hop in for a tea and a chat and forget about all the things I have to do that day. Having a support system from my family has pushed me to continue blogging at times when I was ready to call it quits. Between my family and my significant other, I have a net beneath me strong enough for any fall I might take. They are definitely the main reason that I continue to do what I do. Will there be days when they will drive you up the wall and stress you out even more than your job or blog ever did? Obviously. But don't forget that even in those days, if you were to call them to help you take some photos or read an article you just wrote, they'd be more than happy to do it. That's what family is for, still helping each other out even if they were ripping each other to shreds moments prior!

Do you remember the last time you went out with your friends and didn't take a social media picture of your food or a selfie in the bathroom? When you introduce a new blog into your life it's hard to dissociate from it, especially when you're spending time with your friends. My photo-snapping craziness is now a running joke with all our friends but there are plenty of times when I have to consciously put my camera away and enjoy the time I'm spending with them.

Shameless photo taking for Instagram while everyone waits to eat breakfast. It must be done!

Not every occasion has to be intertwined with blogging In fact, most moments with friends should be just that, friendly moments. Asking a friend to take a few pictures of your outfit (if you're a fashion blogger) is one thing but basically employing them full-time without pay as your photographer is seriously overstepping the boundaries. Make time for your friends whenever you can. Go to the movies, grab some lunch, work out together. Unlike your family, these people choose to be in your life so make sure you choose to be in theirs. If you're going to an event for the blog why not invite your best friend to come with you? Use your blog connections to give you an excuse to see your friends more; if it's not yet paying off monetarily then it can at least give you a way to experience some fun outings that you and your friends would otherwise have not known about. If you can manage to take some weekend trips, do so in a group. Outside of romantic getaways with your partner, catching up with friends on vacation is one of the better things life will has to offer. Nothing will relax you more!

I know it's hard to find a few spare hours in your week, let alone in a day, but if you have an opportunity, I would highly recommend spending that time reading. I have my days when I veg out in front of the television but for the most part a good book always wins. If I am to continue blogging then I must continue writing and a writer should, first and foremost, be well-read. When I'm excited to read a new book, I often tell myself that it is for "research purposes" which takes away any guilt I might have about not spending that time on blogging! While some people's research includes them going to a media library or taking meticulous notes at their computer, mine involves a cup of tea, some PJ's and my favorite new novel of choice.

A collection of all-time favorites. Great for reading and for the occasional Instagram pic ;)

While reading I take mental notes of character developments, writing styles, but mostly I let myself relax and be engulfed in another world: a world that does not include working, or blogging, or networking. I have gotten into the habit of reading before bed whenever I have a chance and the uninterrupted sleep that follows refuels me in unimaginable ways. So welcome the detectives and pirates and flying monkeys into your life– their stories will help create your stories.

Before I started blogging I loved cooking. It wasn't for the sake of having cute posts to share but because I genuinely enjoyed the idea of creating something from scratch that was actually edible and not a pizza pocket. As the blog began to grow, I had lost time and passion for the arts of the kitchen and each time I passed by the area I cringed at the thought of having to do anything but make myself yet another coffee. What I had failed to realize, until much later into my blogging career, was that the time I used to spend cooking and baking was not only a means of sustenance but a meditation of sorts. I would forget for a few brief hours about the rest of my day and would concentrate on something other than what work had to offer. With my stomach grumbling more regularly after hours at the computer, I started to slowly venture back into the kitchen to experiment with recipes I had long since put on hold. The initial few dishes were one hundred percent geared towards a blog post; I would already have set up the camera prior to even starting and knew exactly what the images would entail. I quickly remembered how much I missed my little hobby and to this day I allow myself a few days every week to either bake, cook, or host a full dinner. If you were not big into the idea before, I dare you to give it a shot! You loved creating your blog so think of cooking as another way of creating something; something delicious you can eat, and as a bonus take a million pictures of for social media!

This was delicious. It took approximately forty shots

to fully capture its deliciousness…

When you work most of the week, making time for anything else in your life besides blogging can be a tough nut to crack. There are people to see, books to read, food to cook, and of course the dreaded housework that needs to get done. Chores are enough of a pain when you don't have a blog to run (raise a hand if you love dusting under the bed… Oh look, not one hand in the air…) but when you're already swamped with work they seem like an unnecessary evil; except that they are necessary (and of course very, very evil.) It may seem like a waste of your time to clean out your closet, or do your dishes before the sink looks like you're prepping for a zombie apocalypse, but all these little things still need to get done. Just because you've added blogging to your resume doesn't mean life stops in every other area of your life. I find having a clean house motivates me to work more, and since I work from home, why not keep my office as tidy as possible? You likely will no longer have full days to clean up the messes of the week like you used to but there are still ways to stay on top of household chores before they get out of hand. Break up your chores into parts and do a part a day so that you're not spending hours on housework yet you will still manage to get everything done. Dedicate a bit of time on one day to dusting, another to floors, the next to the dreaded bathroom area and laundry, and before you know it you will be in the habit of always staying on top of things. If you tend to leave dishes in the sink, try to load the dishwasher prior to eating, so when you're done you can get back to blogging or anything else you have planned for the day. When in doubt, call a cleaning service; they are more affordable than you might think and sometimes taking a hit financially is worth it to avoid mental anguish over a filthy home.

Now that your home is clean, are you noticing all the things that are wrong with it? I daily go through areas of our home and think, "This should be here, that should be gone, we need a new something or other". While I can't afford to have the entire place remodeled each month there are definitely small things that can be upgraded or changed that put my fluttery mind at ease. Making time to update your home is a great adventure for a blogger, as it offers not only material for your platform but a "Zenness" to your home that you now share with your business. It might not be affordable to get new furniture but there are always ways to give a space new life without drowning in bills at the end of it.

Deconstruct the areas of your house that need an upgrade. If your kitchen is looking dated, invest in some great new small appliances. These will never feel like frivolous spending as you'll actually put them to good use and most appliances now come in beautiful colors allowing you to display them, rather than hiding them in your cupboards. If you need to give more life to your living room collect some crystal vases and fill them with fresh flowers weekly; nothing screams update like a bowl of new petals.

These days, there are plenty of places to get inexpensive furniture pieces that can be easily updated with a coat of paint and some new hardware. Ikea is a great source for affordable remodeling. And if you're worried about your home looking too much like one of their catalogues, run a search for Ikea hacks. You'll get more options for furniture DIY's than you'll know what to do with.

This vanity set up in my office is basically Ikea dressers and randomly found objects throughout the years.

My partner's mom decorates their cottage with items she finds on the beach. Can we say adorable?

Sometimes all you need to get you more organized and back in love with your home is to re-organize your closet. We forget how much emphasis we should place on our clothes; after all, this is our first impression and a good one opens many doors. A messy closet can lead to frustrating mornings that lead to even more frustrating days. Spend a bit of time getting rid of anything you haven't used in the last two years and anything that looks like it was designed when *Saved by the Bell* was still popular. If it wasn't made in this decade and is not an investment piece, get rid of it. Invest in some closet organizers and some clear shoe boxes and start creating the closet of your dreams. My current closet lives in my office and since I see it every day I am always reminded to keep it tidy, so getting ready is never an issue.

Fashion blogger lifestyle: keep your key pieces out at all times for quicker styling. Also for an emptier looking closet so you have an excuse to buy more stuff you'll only wear once.

A great way to give new life to your abode involves fun outings on the weekends. Garage sales and antique sales are a great way to get pieces you might otherwise not want to splurge on, for a fraction of the cost. My best friend's mom is an avid garage sale goer and you'd be surprised at the number of treasures she finds each time she goes. With a little bit of TLC and some paint, something that was of no use to the person selling it could become the next focal point of your home.

Other than your family and friends, the most important thing you should make time for is yourself. You are the driving force behind this entire operation and without you the world as you know it will crumble and self-destruct! Alright, maybe not that extreme, but you should still give yourself a pat on the back for all you've been able to accomplish and take some time off, when you can, to celebrate that. Vacation, vacation, vacation. I'm not asking you to run to the nearest travel agent and book six months of your life for that unrealistic round-the-world cruise you've always wanted to take (although who knows, maybe one day you'll have time for that), but do try to go on as many getaways as you can afford each year. If your full time job lets you have three weeks of vacation then use them wisely. Incorporate at least one relaxing, "sunny shores" break from the world and maybe a few smaller trips spread evenly throughout the year. Working for a long period of time without any breaks can leave you agitated and frustrated and will have a negative effect on your professional life and on your personal one as well. Think of vacations as going to the sauna after a long workout; it relaxes your mind and muscles and helps you rebuild your energy for the next task. It may seem foolish to tell people to make time for trips but you'd be surprised how many people work non-stop without any breaks at all. Life is much too short to sit at your desk all day and only see the world through a computer screen. Now that you're a blogger, these getaways will fuel your material for the blog; the tans and bikinis are obviously a great bonus!

When you're new to blogging, or even when you've been at it for years, creating blocks of time for anything that isn't blog related can be difficult and your mind will always run back to your blog any chance it gets. It's important to remember that before you were a blogger you were a person, a person with a life and people in that life who mattered and still do. If your blog is not yet making any money then it is just a hobby, and if it bringing in a profit then it is still just a job. There are definitely more important things in life that should not be taken for granted. You don't need to choose between one or the other, much like you do not need to choose between your full time work and your blog; there are ways to find a balance for everything on your to do list. There will be times when some things will get sacrificed for your blog and times when your blog will get sacrificed for your life; it's not the end of the world if any of that occurs.

Some time into running my blog I realized that by creating it I was not just creating a platform for the things I enjoyed in life, I was creating the person that went along with that. I was no longer the scattered girl that forgot her dad's birthday if she didn't put it in her calendar, I was transforming into, well, a grown-up. I had goals and actions planned to make those goals a reality but the only way any of that was to come into fruition was if I stayed positive and mentally aware. Making time for the things that mattered to me, outside of work and blogging, let me do just that. They let me keep who I was before the blogging madness. That girl wasn't so bad, just a lot less focused, and way too obsessed with bad horror movies, but definitely ok to hold on to.

CHAPTER 9

Get Over Yourself

One of the hardest things for me to do as a first time blogger was not taking my blog or myself too seriously. I mean sure, I thought it was the bee's knees and it actually paid for some of the bills, but let's face it, I wasn't launching rocket ships here! Usually, the best way for me to tell if I am doing something extraordinary is to study my mother's face while telling her whatever news I may have. If I was to scream out "Mom, I'm studying to be a doctor!" or "I'm carrying your first grandchild and have just been promoted to lead engineer!" This woman's face would look like a smiling raisin. When I told her I started a blog, I did not see much of a facial difference. Don't get me wrong, she was happy that I was happy but to her point, a blog is not a doctorate or an excuse to buy those stupid-cute baby sneakers. It was then that I realized that I need to tone it down a notch when it comes to how important I think my new venture is, and I learned to laugh at myself in the process.

 Back when I resided in New York I was riding the metro home from work one summer night, sporting my hottest off-the-shoulder number. This thing had cost me a small fortune of hard earned tips and was the darkest shade of lipstick red I've seen (other than Dorothy's slippers.) Having this dress on meant I was more special than I was and with my vintage biker jacket over it, boy, did I feel that! Rush hour on a New York train is no joke, it is usually hot as hell and you're lucky if you can get a breath in without the aid of a ventilator, so when I felt a breeze I was relieved to say the least;

thinking they finally got the fans working. What made me think that after years of near suffocation today would be the day the air conditioning kicked in is beyond me, but I was still relaxed the entire way home, feeling cooler than I had been most of the day. When I reached my stop, and fought my way past a gazillion passengers, an air struck my body that immediately turned on a light bulb. I looked down at my dress in horror and there it was! In the midst of all this rush hour traffic, my left bosom peeking out of my stunning red off the shoulder, just saying hello to the world! So what did I do then? Well, obviously, freak out and run home to tuck my dress to the back of the closet where it did not make another debut until years later. But after a little bit of time I came to realize that while I was embarrassed, what I now had in my arsenal was a great story; one I retell regularly to anyone looking for a good giggle. What's a little exposure on the Q train compared to a lifetime of laughs?

So maybe you've never exposed yourself in public but there are much less drastic ways to, in no better terms, get over your blog. Think of your blog for a minute. Now think of the last blog you saw mentioned on social media, and then the one before that, and so on and so on. There are hundreds of millions of blogs on the internet, so as amazing as your content might be and as snazzy as your life is, there is always someone else doing the exact same thing. Unless you are literally reinventing the wheel on your site, your blog at the end of the day is just that; another blog. That is not to imply that it isn't special, or that it is to be underplayed in any way, but it is also not the root of all existence and it is certainly not the root of your existence. It doesn't define who you are as a person. In fact, keep in mind that you are the one that defines what it is. Don't become that blogger that lives only for their blog; that is both pretentious and redundant. If you're going to redecorate, do it because your house needs an update, not because you want a white fur rug in your office to take pictures on. It's easy to get carried away with how highly we think of blogging, especially when it helps support you, and though it is important, there are always more important things in life. Like catching up on reruns of your favorite show; always make time for that!

Getting over your blog can be tough but getting over yourself can be even tougher. Once blogging opens doors to more experiences, and a closet full of free samples, you might be enticed to think you're better than everyone else who doesn't get the same treatment. I mean, here you are at a red carpet party wearing the newest pair of some brand you love and sipping the finest Chardonnay and they're at home watching TV in their sweats. The message here is clear, right? You've accomplished some form of greatness. Except, not really. While blogging might certainly open a few more doors, if you're in it for the superficial reasons of a long chased dream of fame and fortune not only are you a bad blogger, but you're actually kind of a bad person. Your blog is an extension of who you are so if you want it to be respected, then you need to act as someone that garnishes that respect. Looking down on the people around you lends you no respect at all and greatly harms your reputation as a blogger. It seems like obvious advice (more bees with honey), but you'd be surprised how many people let this newfound attention go to their heads. Don't burn your bridges before you've had a chance to cross them, being a more humble person will make you a much more sought after blogger. Think of it as winning the lottery, you can either be smart with your money and donate some to charity, or you buy yourself a ridiculous amount of stuff and become the joke of your neighborhood. Word gets around so tone it down a notch if you want your blog to keep gaining momentum.

You know that moment in elementary school when the teacher reads out a book passage and asks the class what they thought, and everyone gets their turn to give their opinion? Well, life isn't like that. You don't get to go around raising your hand and telling people what your thoughts are: this is what your blog is for. Your opinions on the blog matter. They matter to you, they matter to your family and friends, and they matter to your readers. Your life outside the blog is a different story. You might be incredibly knowledgeable in the field you're blogging in but opinions outside of your blog are fair play. Everyone will have one, and they will all have their hands up wanting to voice it; sometimes even about your blog. Years in school have prepared us for constructive criticism but when it comes to your blog, the subject may be a tad more sensitive. It's almost like someone calling your baby ugly. What do you do in that case? Logically you accept their critique and part ways so as not to cause a scene, but in your head you have already beaten them to a pulp and strung their head on a stick to warn others about unsolicited advice. "Tell all your friends!" you'd yell, "No one messes with my baby!" Unfortunately there is no red tape for people telling you what they think, and trust me, they will. Sometimes the advice is great and you'll end up going along with it, and sometimes it will be quite the opposite. Either way, listen to what people have to say because as much as your opinion matters, it is not the only one that does.

The other day I walked by a window display full of those "Keep Calm and (insert saying here)" mugs. They had everything from "drinking wine" to "hugging cats" and there it was, amidst the not so fine china collection of cups, with a little picture of a laptop: Keep Calm and Blog On". I almost ran into the store and bought a few for myself and all my friends who have a blog, but ended up walking away for two reasons. First, if I came home with another funny coffee mug we would have to blow out some walls in order to expand our kitchen storage. Second, I keep my blogging calmness in check daily so there's really no need for another reminder. Your blogging career will have ups and downs just like your full time job, the difference with your blog is you are the one that controls the source of the stress. There are no co-workers or bosses to drive you crazy; you're the only one in the office. If something doesn't work out the way you want it to then so be it, the next thing will work out better. Sit down and perform a few breathing exercises, have a sip of coffee from your "Keep Calm" mug, and get back to business. And smile for Christ's sakes! No one likes a sour puss!

Watching old black and white movies always makes me overly sensitive. Not because of the emotional turmoil they usually present but because they honestly make me feel like a terrible person. I watch these people on screen and think, "How are they so satisfied with the smaller pleasures of life and all I can think about is that Chanel bag I need to save for?" This is usually when the realization kicks in that my perspectives in life are skewed. For the few weeks following the movie, I actively attempt to find little pleasures in my everyday life. Whether it's a walk in the park, having a barbeque, or even writing a thank you letter (the note card kind, not some lame email). I do all of the things that I see the black and white, overly-animated film characters do and I must admit, I enjoy my days more fully for that time period. Then life kicks in and I'm back at square one, calling for yet another film to bring me back down to a simpler reality. It seems like an exhausting pattern to have but I found that running a blog can very quickly and crudely lead you to have your head up your bottom. There's always something new to be a part of and sometimes it's nice to remember what really matters. (Not that the Chanel handbag doesn't matter but it might not be as high of a priority as it seems to be when you're flipping through your Instagram feed.)

Whenever time allows it, take a step back and reevaluate how seriously you take your blogging career. While we are all definitely doing something creative and out of the niche (or as out of the niche as we can be with a new blog being created every second), we are still at the end of the day just people with two jobs and an opinion. If you're going to do one meditation per day, make sure it's one that makes you chill the heck out. Calm your nerves and get over yourself.

Your blog, your job, and everyone in your life will thank you for it. So throw on your symbolic red off the shoulder dress, pull down the left side, and ride the subway all day! After two round trips I'm sure everything will come into perspective.

ACKNOWLEDGMENTS

No man is an island and I am very much just a tiny boat in the sea without some of these very important people that have helped make this book a reality.

To my family, thank you for being so supportive. I know I didn't turn out to be a doctor but you've helped me in all of my endeavors no matter how trivial they may have been. Dad, thank you for spending weeks building those tables with me for that "photography" project back in my misunderstood teen angst days. A special thanks goes out to my mom who has not stopped talking to me even though I used her quotes in this book. Love you!

To my partner in crime, Scott. You are by far the best life partner a crazy girl can ask for. Thank you for letting me read the chapters to you ad nauseum and helping me get through this with minimal hiccups. Also, don't think I don't appreciate all the times you've taken my stupid outfit pictures when all you wanted to do was hang out. You have given me a home full of love and laughter and let me keep my clothes in every closet. How could any girl ask for more?

To my editors, Lexie Sage and Shelley D'Souza. None of this would be possible without your immense help. Thank you for helping transform this work into a reality. It would be nothing but rambled words on a page without your dedicated help. Lexie, I have you on a lifetime supply of pink markers for future edits. They have made this book and my life complete.

My photographer and closest friend, Chris Vassalos; you have pushed me to want more for the blog, for this book, and for my life as a whole. You are truly a master of your craft so thank you for making me feel like a princess every time we were on set.

To all my friends, I know I'm a pain but you stuck around anyhow and that's the most I could ever ask for. A special thanks to my bestie Lindsay for being such an amazing shoulder to cry on and a party to laugh with. You are my adopted family so there is no escape for you now!

Finally, to all of my readers both of this book and of the blog. Thank you for all of your support, comments, and picture likes. You are the reason I continue to do this and I appreciate every single one of you in unimaginable ways.

RESOURCES

Useful sites I regularly use for my personal blog work, links to referenced materials and generally cool sites to check out.

BLOG PLATFORMS:

www.squarespace.com

The platform I use for my blog. Easy to navigate and very user and commerce friendly.

www.wordpress.com

Great optimization for blogging. Has great features for affiliate marketing and is well recognizable in the industry.

www.blogger.com

Runs on very easy to use templates and can connect to Google+ and Google AdSense with ease. A great feature of this platform is it allows you to post from any device.

ONLINE DELEGATION:

www.hootsuite.com

Great for all of your online delegation needs. Comes with tutorials to get you up to speed on the program. Basically a time-saving genius on the go.

www.mailchimp.com

The best option for creating newsletters and staying in touch with your readers. Has a free option which is more than sufficient for beginners and offers paid upgrades for users with high subscription levels.

www.flipboard.com

A customized magazine for your mobile device. Great app to use as a secondary source to upload your articles to and can be used to drive traffic to your blog platform.

www.feedly.com/i/welcome

Similar to Flipboard but much nicer for your battery life.

PHOTOGRAPHY AND VIDEO:

www.pixabay.com

One of the largest libraries of free copyright friendly images available for downloading. Images are available to download in a variety of sizes which makes this site perfect for online and print use.

www.adobe.com

Every program you need to edit your photography and video on a professional level.

www.sonycreativesoftware.com/vegaspro

My personal favorite for video editing. Easy to understand (comparable to the industry standard) and can be used for beginner video editing as well as novices of the craft.

www.bhphotovideo.com

Fantastic selection of online photo and video supplies and equipment. The prices are competitive for the industry and shipping is quite speedy.

STATIONARY AND OFFICE:

www.smythson.com

For all of your agenda needs. A variety of finishes and colors available and the product is made of high quality materials, so it will sustain a lot of wear and tear.

www.zazzle.com

A good source of business card designs and affordable business card printing services. You can create anything from minimal to gold leafed cards. The company offers customization for other items such as stationary and clothing.

www.theghostlystore.com/collections/behance-action-method

If you need help organizing your life, these notebooks use the action method to help tasks get maintained.

www.tigerdirect.com

An absolute favorite of mine for tech needs.

BLOG TOOLS:

www.huffingtonpost.com

Offers the best traffic for your guest blogging. In order to be accepted as a blogger you must submit a fully written story pitch and be approved by the editorial team.

www.rafflecopter.com

This site will help you take the stress out of your next giveaway. Options include Pinterest integration, email newsletters, winner picker, and a multitude of others depending on which package is selected.

https://adwords.google.com/KeywordPlanner

Helps with SEO and general research for your keyword searches. A great tool to use prior to selecting titles for your posts.

READING:

www.texture.com

An app geared to provide digital copies of all of your favorite magazines for a monthly price. Takes the bulk of magazine copies out of your bag and allows for a more affordable reading experience.

INSPIRATIONAL AND FUN:

www.estatesales.net

A list of all current estate sales based on your postal code.

www.pinterest.com

A photo based app geared towards inspirational information. An easy to navigate platform that allows you to save images you enjoy for later viewing as well as add your own images to your profile.

www.hometalk.com

Very similar to Pinterest but geared towards home décor and interior design.

www.wanelo.com

Stands for Want, Need, Love. This app lets you shop directly from your phone. You can follow your favorite stores and curate your personalized mall.

www.fitnessblender.com

A huge selection of free online workouts for whatever mood you're in.

SAMPLES OF MY FAVORITE POSTS

Not Just a Boys Club, May 13

Those who know me will vouch that I am not the daintiest creature. I have never been attracted to overly feminine objects and much to my mother's disappointment I believe I am borderline allergic to being ladylike. This somewhat rough behaviour has heavily influenced the way I put myself together; the idea of appearing overly girly sends shivers down my spine. When it comes to jewelry, my attitude is no different; I would rather sport pieces that look like I ripped them off my boyfriend than something frilly and overly feminine. This is where my growing love for **Vitaly jewelry** fits in.

I have recently come across the brand in a shop in the east end during a lazy Sunday afternoon. While browsing through racks of clothes my eye hungrily gravitated towards the Vitaly display at the front counter. Arranged on a wood board, the pieces looked like perfect little appetizers and although I was on a shopping diet I could not help myself but look. Despite my better efforts, it was snack time!

What attracted me most were the industrial elements in all of the pieces. Elements that were not overpowering, as is the case for most other unisex jewelry, but work in perfect balance with their shape and size. The rings are simple with just the right amount of detail, carrying all of the punch of a massive statement piece without being overly heavy making them impeccably suited for boys and girls alike. As I slipped into the Protegir pendant I ended up purchasing I felt like Cinderella putting on a glass slipper. It was an effortless fit. I think this is the best way to describe these collections; they are easy to wear pieces that will definitely get you noticed.

So it looks like I am undoubtedly off my diet and thanks to Vitaly's brilliant designs I will be overweight in the jewelry department in no time. Keep those pieces coming boys because this girl can't get enough of them!

Springing It, Apr 18

Spring is finally in Toronto and I'm coming out of hibernation and with it I'm bringing out my spring layers. Everywhere I go I see messaging of the summer to come but I'd like to take the time to acknowledge the season that does not get much recognition. Sure it doesn't have the chalet sports of winter, or the lush colored leaves of fall, and it most definitely does not boast bikinis like summer but springtime is a great season if you love your layers. This is the perfect time of the year to give your dull winter sweaters a final spin in a fun, non-fussy way.

Though it's not warm enough to don your short sleeves and minis (although today was a lovely exception) it is definitely warm enough to move on to lighter trenches and thinner scarves and heels that don't make your legs buckle from walking on icy streets. It is also the perfect time to break out those bags you love that can't sustain the winter months and aren't large enough to hold your mittens, and muffs, and general cold weather gear. Can we say good riddance?

For this look I opted for a lighter sweater with large side splits (no under tank needed because it's warm as hell) and faux leather roll up joggers. Since I did still need a coat I went with a light grey thin wool blazer trench which is warm enough to keep me comfortable but not so thick that I hate wearing it. I went with a simple uni-scarf that can be unrolled easily if I get too heated and is easy enough to carry around if it needs to be removed. For a pop of texture I chose these absolutely fab leopard print kitten heel booties, these are my favorite go to's for this in between weather as they're comfortable enough to walk in all day but still look fun and elevate the outfit. When I think of bags I can never get sick of wearing, the crossbody comes to mind and this camel leather **Gucci horsebit** is no exception. It holds just enough necessities to get me through the day and is light enough that I don't feel like I have a purse full of bricks, which is pretty standard for me I'm afraid. For an added detail, I finally have a sunny excuse to wear my sunglasses, a very quick and easy way to dress up any outfit.

So no more winter blues for this girl that's for sure. Adios snow, goodbye slush, and see you later windy days! This chicken has sprung into spring with every inch of her body, hope you're all enjoying this long awaited season as much as I am!

An Island Entire of Itself, Apr 19

It had been years since I experimented with using myself as a subject for my own photography. It seemed so much easier to go through with these projects when I was much younger and more self-assured without the sheepishness I've seemed to develop with age. As the years passed, I found myself becoming more introverted when it came to standing in front of a lens and pretending it isn't there, after all, it very much was there; watching me with its one judging eye. And so the projects grew smaller in their scope and their numbers dwindled until I was safely tucked away behind the scenes for every photograph I took.

This year however something changed, as though I had taken a trip to Oz and came back much braver than I had left, proudly brushing my mane and ready to jump in the spotlight, or more realistically inch myself closer to it one toe at a time. With my head higher than it has been in quite some time I unfolded my very dusty tripod and thought "today is the day for selfies". It sounds very silly considering how many of those we take with our phones daily but to photograph yourself in a controlled setting without a cellular safety is quite a different experience, even though there's no one there with you it really feels as though someone is behind the camera watching you and instructing you how to pose. It is as if you are both in your body and out of it all at the same time having an interaction between the two, like playing chess with yourself and flipping the board around for every turn.

    I won't lie, the experience was nerve-wrecking and I did feel quite foolish at first but towards the end of the session I accepted my fate and managed to stop thinking about what the entire charade must look like. I think the next step in my self-proclaimed photo therapy is moving the shoot to a public location. I can probably Photoshop my beet-red face in post-production.

Independent Spirit, Aug 30

I think the sign of a good city is the amount of entrepreneurship one can come across in the realm of retail. Be it boutiques or cafes or bars, if you find yourself surrounded by start-ups you are sure to stick around for a while. Toronto has not always been as eclectic as it has now become but it seems to have grown wings overnight, or at least ruffled its feathers and made a move in the right direction. One thing is certain; our little city is booming. Being a huge supporter of the entrepreneur spirit I am always excited to meet others who work towards keeping individuality alive within the walls of our city which is why it was so exciting to have a behind the scenes look at the Fall '15 collections for Sashion; a team that works only with independent designers.

The event was almost a mix of a fashion shoot, boutique store front, and café. All three were executed to perfection. The attention to detail was tremendously carried out throughout the entire space. There were hints that led back to Sashion spread throughout which helped keep the event grounded. The shoot took place in an east end studio, a beautiful space I would have loved to convert into a live/work area. Catering involved perfect little batches of rice pudding that you could garnish with several choices of toppings, a coffee station, and the cutest cartons of Box Water.

And now to the best part, the fashion of course. The selection for the fall lines was impeccable. It was easy to see that they were carefully picked to fit the aesthetic of Sashion but also offer some good choices for a wider range of personal preference. I immediately gravitated towards the structured minimal pieces. The shoot itself was close to being a performance piece. It took place almost behind clear glass with all of the attendees watching the changes in outfits and last minute preps. A very clever way to show people the new collection and keep the event interesting and not pretentious.

In the end, I hopped on the streetcar and rushed back to go through some of the images from the day. The ride back was shorter than expected since I spent most of it going through the Sashion website and making my wish list. Flowers in hand (a gift from the team) I couldn't help but think what if every web based retail store worked this hard to empower the individual designer? How much bigger would Toronto's footprint be in the world of fashion?

Danish Girl in Toronto, Sept 24

To film or not to film? The ongoing question on my mind every year when TIFF is on the horizon. There are always a few main productions I want to see and more often than not I end up going to see the smaller independent films not only because I whole heartedly support smaller business ventures but because those are the ones that end up tugging at my emotions like a basket full of kittens. This year was no different and I must say I am glad I avoided the Johnny Depp and Jake Gyllenhaal crowds to instead go see The Danish Girl.

Where do I even begin? The fact that one can watch a film in a massive theatre, seated on red velvet chairs on a balcony is still baffling my mind. The experience itself was truly heightened by the location chosen to air the film, in this case the Princess of Wales theatre. The film itself was incredible starting at the cinematography and ending with the acting. I truly did not believe that a subject matter that I cannot relate to on a personal level could cause so much emotional turmoil (I was in between tears and laughter the entire airing). The acting was superior to say the least and every character found a way to become relatable on a human level minutes into the showing, a feat that I find takes much longer in most other recent films I have watched.

In the end, I walked out with slightly puffier eyes than I walked in with and a new found appreciation for the human spirit. So my question for the year is answered; to film! To film even if my schedule does not allow it. To film because an hour and a half of watching became the truly most remarkable hour and a half of my entire year.

ABOUT THE AUTHOR

Born in Moscow, Russia, Inessa Radostin has grown up as a travelling fanatic due to the large influence of her parents and their continuous relocation. Upon settling in Canada, Inessa began her professional career in the photography business creating and operating *Namelings*, a gallery and café hybrid.

Inessa's love of fashion has pushed her to follow her passion into the retail stream where she continued to run several large Canadian retailers and store fronts. In March of 2015, Inessa created her self-titled blog highlighting various topics that piqued her interest.

What began as a place to share fashion choices and personal favorites has evolved to include reviews, styling collaborations and brand affiliations. Her appreciation for photography, inherited from her father, has led Inessa to expand the blog into a business model allowing for photography services and brand design.

As an immense supporter of emerging talent within the fashion and beauty sector, Inessa has continued to mentor young start-up businesses specializing in blog maintenance and creation.

Inessa is in the process of expanding the blog to include interior design and webinars for new writers.

Inessa Radostin currently resides in Toronto, Ontario.

AUTHOR LINKS

www.inessaradostin.com

www.instagram.com/inessaradostin

www.facebook.com/people/Inessa-Radostin/100009105835620

www.twitter.com/inessaradostin

www.youtube.com/channel/UCNgU4x0tIpvvI4ixMDlS7TQ

www.pinterest.com/inessaradostin

www.huffingtonpost.ca/inessa-radostin

FASHION CREDITS

Page 7

Headphones by SuperSonic

Page 24

Watch by DKNY

Rings by Michael Kors, Aldo

Page 30

Agenda by inSidegift

Page 34

Bag by Gucci

Boots by Zara

Pants by H&M

Page 46

Dress by Forever21

Sandals by Guess

Page 47

Bathing suit by Greenlee

Clutch by Estee Lauder

Sunglasses by YSL

Bracelets by Pura Vida

Sandals by Adidas

Page 54

T-shirt by Forever21

Sunglasses by Forever21

Pants by H&M

Bag by Aimee Kestenberg

Sneakers by Boemos

Page 73- Page 82

Top by Nike

Pants by Under Armour

Bra by Calvin Klein

CPSIA information can be obtained
at www.ICGtesting.com
Printed in the USA
FSOW03n1250301116
28004FS